Growth

Linwood Jackson, Jr.

© Copyright 2020, Linwood Jackson, Jr.

All Rights Reserved.

No part of this book may be reproduced, stored in a retrieval system, or transmitted by any means, electronic, mechanical, photocopying, recording, or otherwise, without written permission from the author.

ISBN: 978-1-60414-974-6

Cover art and design by Fatima Azhar

For more information,
email the author at LinwoodJackson@hotmail.com,
or visit linwoodjacksonjr.com

Published by
Fideli Publishing, Inc.
www.FideliPublishing.com

We, when it comes to who we are and should be,
look for acceptance, worth, appreciation, validation, confidence,
and love from every thing and one,
Never considering that acknowledgment
can only come from within.

We already possess what we look for.
The issue is in learning how to access what we possess.

Every one of us is born with a "spouse."
This "spouse" is the spirit, character, or mind of our being.
If we should have satisfactory equilibrium, our "spouse," or the
mind of our inward person, must receive unadulterated affection.

By allowing our inward person to begin to feel and to comprehend its age, an internal awareness develops, allowing it to then challenge our character. This conflict causes our character to learn the awareness our inward person is experiencing, causing the drama of one coming to learn how to marry their own self to begin.

The greatest drama of the ages is held within, and he or she tuning in will receive the greatest reward for their performance, even a character that is able to edify every eye observing it.

Define love. Define love to no one, and to no thing, but to you. Define love and challenge it. Define love and edify it. Define love and practice it. Define love, and be.

L

Table of Contents

The Apple 1
To Construct 4
Remember Me 7
Still 10
Treasure 13
Learn 18
Until The Time 21
Blessedness 24
You Are Contrary 26
The Means 28
Communion 30
As I Am 33
Appear 36
Return 38
Waiting 41
Continue 43
You 46
Love Me 48
I Prayed 51
Acknowledgment 53
An End 55
Clarification 58
Rare 60
Union 65
Consider 67
Know 69
To Wisdom 74
Stop 79
Say 81
Growth 85
See 88
Exist 93

The Apple

I would be a fool to waste you,
I would be a fool to neglect you,
For if I never comfort you,
Then I deserve death,
And if I forget to lay with you,
Better had it been if I was never born.
Your father is beside himself,
He is gone mad,
Mad to have ever let you go.
Your father is a daring man,
He is strong in heart,
Strong to ever trust you with me.
I therefore praise him:
He has my respect.

For the manner of your virtue,
The tongue of your body,
The texture of your skin,
The frame of your structure,
The dress of your substance,
The essence of your matter,
The language of your adornment,
And for the tone of your eyes,
I will never betray him.
I will go over what he has done,
I will know what he has perfected,
My hands will learn his beauty,
I will have intercourse with his voice,
I will console his thoughts,
She will be safe in my arms.

I therefore praise him,

I will praise him for the work of his hands,
I will praise him for the power of his force,
I will praise him for his tenderheartedness,
And I will love her as she loves him,

And I will love him,
Even as I know that he loves me,
Because he gave me his love,
And his love cherishes me.

How can a man not know what he has?
How can a man ignore what he needs?
And what he knows he needs,
When found without that necessity,
Should a man ignore the void within?

Must a coat suffocate all things?
Can a mask hide the body?
How vain is the eye?
How strange is the heart?
How numb is the perception?
And concerning a right constitution,
What is it?

I will die without her.
My breath is vain when apart from her.
My flesh will eat me if I don't know her,
And if I never hug her,
Better had it been if I was never born.

The apple of the eye of my father,

Of my father in law,
She is my life,
And is also the death of me.
Her taste consumes me,
Her fragrance shuts me up,
Her touch stills me,
Her hair keeps me the entire night,
And her voice kills the day away.

The apple of the eye of my father,
Of my father in law,
She is my wife,
And I love her.

To Construct

Why construct a woman?
What is that "good" in crafting a wife?
How can she live through a man?
How can a man check her thoughts?
Must a man rule a woman?
Is a wife a slave to her husband?
If she is made by her man,
Is not he then become the woman?
Is not she then become a man?
What is her voice?
Is it not male?
And as we hear her,
Is he not become female?
And her form,
Fully delineated,
Is not her structure his?

Her structure is not hers.
She is no woman.
Although she may appear to be,
She is but male,
And her structure is a desired reality.
Can he give her life?
Must her breath come from his?
And can he supply her soul?
Doesn't her life become his life?
And if he gives her life,
It is not she, who functions,
But rather he is in her.

So as she moves,
Is it not his figure we admire?
And the light of her presence,
Is it not his shadow?
She is not her own,
She owns no thing of her self,
She is but a pattern of a thought,
And every thing she should claim,
Every thing she should feel,
Every ambition,
Every fabric of her clothes,
Every emotion,
Every ache in her heart,
She will know only by his mind,
For her power is no power at all,
And her glory is no glory at all.

She is a waste.
Her existence is fraudulent.
Her beauty is no beauty at all,
Her fragrant demeanor is flesh.
O how my heart burns for her!
She does not know her birth,
And I would never tell her,
But I would remove her from him,
And I would help her.

What then is virtue?
What is to be praised?
What is full of value?
What is beyond elegance?
Why bless originality?

Many women are bound by lust,
Many women are abused,
And when they suffer,
Is it not their men that suffer?
Are not her sufferings his?
When she cries,
Is it not because he first hurts?
When she is broken?
Is it not because he is shattered?
Is not her abuse his?
Are not his wounds hers?

Is not a crafted wife a forced idea?
Is not a crafted wife self-violation?
A husband and a wife are one,
And in that oneness they are separated,
Separated to know each other as individuals,
For they met as individuals,
And as individuals they exist as one.

Remember Me

Why do I know humiliation?
Am I strange just for my self?
Have I desired any one else?
Or have I lied to you?

If I should toss and turn forever,
Time would fail me for your dispute.
If "ever" should allow me into its realm,
"Ever" would beg for release from my conviction.
How precious is heartbreak then?
How warm is a fever?
How gross is negligence?
How I have grown so violent,
How I have become so depressed,
For the bond of your chain,
And for the kiss of your flame,
And for the depth of your ocean,
And for the lock of your chest,
Is sincerely beyond me.

Would I act without consent?
Should I study you with you knowing?
How can I explain you without instruction?
Who then has taught me of you?
Why should I proceed,
As though deeply instructed,
After a knowledge of you,
And after your matter,
If I was forbidden to,
Or if your father said, "No."

Am I beside myself?
Have I not cared for my eyes?
Are not your arms ever around me?
Have we not lain and exchanged fragrances?
Have we not fought,
And have we never struggled,
Only to grow closer?
Can I search without a thought?
Is contemplation born from nothing?
What is heaviness of the heart?
Should I never open up to you?
Was I absent when you were broken?
Did I run when you were cruel?
Did I overreact when you were alarmed?
Did I fight your need for space?
Did I ignore your counsel?
Every thing you put before my face,
Did I not eat it quietly?
And as I ate,
Did you not smile from my smile?
And have you never threatened my life,
Concerning if I should eat from another table?
And of your tears,
Of the long nights awake until the light,
Shed for your Country,
And for your mother,
And for the reproach of your father,
Did I not press you to make me know your pain?
Did I ever fail to reason with you?
Has there ever been a moment,
Where fear kept me from you,
Or where my pride abused you?

I should die if I ever know another,
For no woman is as my wife.
I have,
That the ring of my sobriety may encircle her voice,
Chosen to suffer for her.

Blessed is your father,
O my wife of his spirit.
If by bitterness I may gain your attention,
Then may your attention console my endeavor.

Still

I do praise your father,
Because he gave me you,
And to have you,
I know many deaths.

I praise him for his kindness,
I thank him for thinking of me,
For when I gave him me,
Then he gave me you,
And when I fought for me,
When I died for life,
He knew I would die for you,
He knew I would live for you.

I will live for you,
And I will die for you,
Because I live for your father,
And I die for your father.
I praise him for giving your hand in marriage,
I love him more because of you,
And my love will overflow for you:
I will care for his daughter.

I will fight for your affection,
I will know your kiss,
I will protect you with my life,
I will die for you,
Because you also suffer for me.

I am not a fool to ignore your heart.
As I prepared for you,
Never knowing who you were,

I am not stubborn to ignore your past.
As he was raising me,
He was preparing you for me,
Even though you did not know me.
I am not a beast against your labor,
I will not be cruel against your spirit,
For you were told to be right,
You were taught to be still,
You were pained by bitterness,
And endured for a soul you didn't know.

Who knows a virtuous woman?
I should sound insane to speak of you.

To mention your smile,
To speak of your walk,
To talk of your fury,
To describe your voice,
To pronounce your heart,
To confess your arms,
To proclaim your eyes,
To tell of your hair,
To explain your hands,
To narrate your legs,
To prove your table,
To admit your jealousy,
Who would believe me?

All who hear of you will love you.
All who hear you will love your father.
You are his image,
You are his voice in form,

You are his portrayed throne,
Your beauty is the crown of his fame.

Blessed is your father,
Who,
For years,
Saw me alone,
Who heard me cry out for loneliness,
Who watched me behave perversely,
Yet never left me,
But did consider my plea for recovery.
Blessed is your father,
And blessed are you.
I love life because of you,
I know stillness because of our marriage.

Treasure

My wife once told me,
The voice of my house once said,

"Is there any thing above knowledge?
What is better than understanding?
Your speech may be perfect,
Your dress may be sincere,
Your person may know order,
But without pure reason,
And without sound philosophy,
Without a sure heart,
And with no intelligent spirit,
Your stomach will fail,
And your eyes will fall out.

"What were you before me?
And if we never met,
Would I even have life?
I am for you,
Even as you are for me;
But were you not asleep before me?
Wasn't I far from your mind?

"Did you not argue incorrectly?
Weren't your thoughts scattered?
Did you not drink up self-violation?
Were you not thirsty?
I knew you only in nakedness,
I knew you first in plague,
And this is why he raised me for you,
This is why your breath supports me.

"I am yours,
And before you knew me,
I sat under my mother and learned,
And I sat under my father and heard,
The message to give to my husband,
And the law to feed my children.

"Before you knew me,
And before our eyes met,
I existed when time only knew love,
And when death was only a legend.

"Before you knew me,
And before we touched,
When my father spoke all things into existence,
And when he brought all things into being,
When every thing knew benevolence,
When all things spoke his language,
There I received instruction from him,
And also counsel from my mother:
They fed me their mind,
And I digested their compassion.
I remained honest for my husband,
I remained quiet for my time,
For my sisters had husbands,
And they too had children,
But I would know no man,
I would go only where I was sent,
And I would only love who I knew appreciated me.

"I am my father's daughter,
And I love my father.

I was there when he gave his voice life,
I was there to examine him,
For I knew him,
And I knew the place where his voice went:
I spoke to every thing wherein his voice went,
And I learned about love.

"Knowledge is not knowledge,
And understanding is not prideful,
For wisdom is life's principle,
And wisdom's love escapes knowledge.

"I sat in the clouds,
I slept in the earth,
I spoke to the creatures,
I climbed the trees.
I drank the rain,
I swam in the ocean,
I took lightning in my hand,
I studied thunder,
I stood in fire,
I studied matter.
I heard His intention,
I saw his angels,
I observed his kindness,
I felt the world's robe,
I played in the snow,
I observed the mountains,
I ran in every open field,
I tasted the air.
I busied myself with his doctrine,
My course was his law,

"My father gave my sisters away,
And they were wise for their men,
And he did have men for me,
But their spirit was not yours.
He perfected me for you,
And he protected me for you,
For while he perfected you for me,
And while you suffered what you did,
I quietly waited for you,
Because I would make your heart believe.

"My husband,
Know me.
My man,
Commune with me.
Consider my doctrine,
Comprehend my law,
For my thoughts are not mine,
And my beauty is inherited:
He has given me my form,
And my mother has blessed it.

"I am my father's daughter,
I have penetrated his mind,
And I am yours so that you may know him:
He gave you me so that you may be his son by a law.

"I love your touch,
Handle me.
I am comforted by your voice,
Know me.
All things may fill every thing,
All things may examine and determine all things,
But all things have no end,
And every thing is fraudulent,
If it does not plunge into my father's will,
And if it doesn't know his love,
Which is a love that passes knowledge.

"If knowledge serves for no change,
And if science does not comfort,
What good is understanding?
I am your wife,
And I am not yet perfect,
For our Father has created us for perfection,
And He has married us for a good work."

Learn

My wife once said to me,
The joy of my spirit once taught,

"Humility nourishes better than food,
Simplicity upholds all.

"Quiet your heart and earn knowledge,
Still your thoughts and know sense,
Refrain from eating your heart,
Administer discretion against your self,
And retain wisdom and understanding.

"Let your soul thin for a better appointment,
Befriend bitterness for favor,
For who can tell,
From one day to the next,
How long our life will be?
"Who can believe,

And who can trust,
That every moment is preserved,
And that time will pity us?

Extend life by a teachable demeanor:
Learn how to hear,
Learn how to keep,
Learn how to employ,
That your years may never end,
And that we may never be separated.
Because I sat under my mother,
And because my father raised me,
Do not be stubborn towards me.
Love me

And consider my advice.

"My name is wisdom and rain,
My skin is covered with a custom robe,
Even a garment created by my father,
And my mother's law is my soft flesh.
My two feet bear my father's law,
My hair reveals the glory of his Majesty.

"There is labor in every thing:
Know employment for health,
Know labor for strength.
Eat every thing that I give you,
For before you knew me,
And before our eyes met,
My father told me,

'Feed your husband and know him,
Hear his thoughts and bear with him.
You will be to him a home,
He will be to you a band,
And as long as your warmth is sure,
As long as your communion is sound,
Your voice will command his love,
And his voice will bind you to him.

'Blessed is the man that finds you,
Blessed is the bed that you will share.
You are his life.
Your blood is to be devoured,
Your jewel is to be treasured,
For your spirit will shake his earth,
And your form will consume his beauty.

'Blessed is the man that waits for you,
Blessed is he that loves you,
For you will elevate him,
You will perfect his name,
And by you he will live.
By your instruction he will never die.'

"My husband, I speak no error.
What have I to gain by falsehood?
Is not your death mine?
Am not I bound to you?
Is not your heart the same as mine?
Would I destroy myself?
Should I put my father to shame?
Should I waste my mother's tongue?

"Hush,
And reserve your thoughts.
Know the heritage of my father,
Digest the recipes of my mother.
Because silence is better than wealth,
Meekness is great with reverence,
Mortification procures betterment,
And that benefit increases life.

"In all things,
And with every thing,
Learn science and obtain wisdom,
Cultivate skill and earn faith,
Learn discipline to perfect fear:
Carefully improve your manners."

Until The Time

I am thankful to my God for you,
And because you are His wisdom's daughter,
Because you are the dress of its form,
I will protect our home,
I will never violate you.

My body would turn to water,
My well would run dry,
My sky would contract,
I would vanish into nothing,
If I ever hurt your eyes.
Why should I scar you?
Why should I offend?
If you die, don't I?
If you are distressed, am I not?
I cannot bear your eyes,
And I will not entertain your sorrow,
From my own ignorance,
My own thoughtlessness,
From my own neglect,
For some irreverent failure in me,
In me to know you,
And to hear you,
Since I love you.

And I love your father.
I met you already while knowing you,
Yet being lame,
I did not correctly introduce myself,
And while I managed error,

And while seduced by other women,

I gave many women attention,
I handled many parts and organs,
I lived under various instruments,
And you saw it all,
Remaining silent until the time.
But I grew tired of them,
As you knew I would,
For their bodies were cruel,
Their voices were unbearable,
They were flesh while I was not,
And I ate them while I was not,
I drank them in nothingness:
I had intercourse with corpses.

You knew what I didn't know,
But you couldn't say what I didn't see,
And it was done to help my heart,
In that I may open up to what is real,
That I may open up to me.
I have been exposed to you,
But you aren't afraid of me.
Only you know me,
But you aren't afraid of me.
When the time was right,
And when the season appeared,
I saw your face,
And when I saw your tears for me,
It was then that I did feel for me.
When we died together,

When we wept on each other,
I told you that I only wanted you,
And you spoke with me,
You gave me your heart,
And I married your thoughts to my spirit.
I begged your father for your hand,
I aggravated my God for you,
And I will always annoy him for my desire,
Even for the wife of my soul,
The mother of my children,
The rain of my cloud,
The mind of my purpose,
That I may win you,
And that I may love you,
As ought.
I thank my God for you,
Even for the kindness of his heart.
He gave me a wife,
And her mind excels her form,
But her form excels her mind,
And her body is mine,
And my limbs are hers.

Blessed is your father and our wisdom,
And what he has brought together,
Let us establish it for ever.

Blessedness

My wife,
The ageless darling of my fascination,
The limitless bounty of my strength:
Is it better to feel you or to hold you?
Is it better to embrace you or to experience you?
Is it better to discern you or to cradle you?
Is it better to fondle you or to taste you?

You are not flesh,
But I do live in flesh,
And you do keep our house,
Along with the members therein,
But I do live in flesh,
And you are of another force.

If I only existed as flesh,
How miserable would I be?
I have existed as flesh,
I have told you my death,
And how miserable was I?
Yet, my wife,
The love of my youth,
You are for the mind and not for the body,
And without you I am foul.
You are my balance,
Without you I am unbalanced,
With you equilibrium is redefined,
For a symmetrical body is agony to the inward person,
But self-control and self-possession is right.

Yet I am in flesh,
I know no thing but sensation,
Which is why your father gave me to you.
As flesh, I am carnal,
And as flesh has flesh,
Am I wrong to want you as flesh?

Am I wrong?
You have heard me say this before.
Your face changes when you hear this,
But I am flesh,
It is all that I am.
You have instructed me to think higher,
You have instructed me to ignore ease,
But I am flesh,
I love you knowledgeably,
I do not care to pervert you,
But there is a mind within this body that is natural,
And this is why I love you,
Because,
To me,

You Are Contrary

Your arrows shoot,
They shoot and hit,
They hit and never miss,
Taking me.

If the sting of death is sin,
Then the sting of life is desire,
The desire to know,
And to look for,
And to search after,
And to incline towards,
And to investigate,
For examination.
You are life,
Your influence is learning,
Your kiss is in understanding,
And because you also share my mind,
You consent to ravaging,
Even to passionate intercourse,
Which is a normal wife's contrition.

If you were not blessed,
If you were not so delightful,
My heart would not ache for you,
I would know no death for you,
But your voice,
The way of your order,
The organization of your form,
I would have,
Base or noble.
Yet I thank my God,
Who is our Counselor,
Because you,
Being wholly noble,
Educate me,
Who is naturally unruly.

The Means

My wife,
The darling of my heart,
She who adds comfort to my mind,
She who warms my perception,
She who is my inspiration,
She who owns my love,
Who is the one instructing my kindness,
The one counseling my charity,
The woman dressing my ignorance,

I am nothing without her voice,
But within her I am sound.
I am a body of chemicals,
I am a body of energy,
I am a body of injury,
But she is my sanctuary,
She is my body of reason,
She is the reason of my body.

This body,
Her body,
The body of my spouse,
Is without manipulation,
Because she is life,
And by her breath I live.
Through her breath I matter,
And because of her breath I care.

Hold my thoughts,
My spouse and my love,
Console my feelings,
My spirit and my wife,

That I may learn of your love,
That I may learn of it to love you,
That I may learn of your sensitivity,
That I may learn of it to love my self.
Give me your love,
Give me the frame of your mind,
Give me the direction of your hope,
Surrender your body,
Spread your *self*,
Let me in to your arms,
That I may know how to comfort,
And let me into your mind,
That I may care for self's good.

By you,
I know only love.
By you,
I know gratitude.
So give me your praise,
Teach me how to please you,
Teach me how to serve you,
And I will never stop,
I will never put off my duty,
My responsibility to you,
My wife,
The soul of my spirit,
The power of my conscience,
The means of my being.

Communion

I know only pain because of you.
My heart hurts for your form.
I have you today,
And I'll have you tonight,
But then we part,
And I am left sorry,
Unable to rationalize my world.
Tonight I have you,
And tomorrow I hold you,
But then we part,
Becoming contemporaries,
Yet individual to life's context.

My inwards burn for your breath,
My mouth thirsts for your taste,
My body itches for your moisture,
My limbs miss your members.
You are not always here,
As I am not always there,
And I hope you know my fear,
I hope you know my desire,
I hope you feel my loss.

I pray you know my fever,
I hope you feel our separation,
I hope you know my mind,
So that you can know my love,
So that you can see my honesty.

I hope you die of sorrow,
I hope you are sick of love,
When we are not together,
When we are apart.
I hope that you die of a broken heart,
I hope that you are grieved,
When you are alone,
When you are without me,
As I know only depression,
And gloom,
When I am without you.

I hope you know my love,
That it is deeper than the sea,
That it is wider than the sky,
As intelligent as the universe.
I hope you know my love,
I hope you understand my affection,
That it is deeper than flesh,
That it is as bountiful as the air,
And as infinite as kindness.

When we are apart,
I hope you fail of life,
I hope misery surrounds you,
I hope depression consumes you,
I hope anxiety covers you,
I hope need worries you.
I hope you know this love,
So that the next time we meet,
And the next time we speak,
We may soberly embrace,

My wife,
My heart,
The joy of my conscience,
Never leave me,
Never be quiet.

My wife,
My heart,
The life of my conscience,
When we are apart,
I hope you know the pain I feel,
So that when we meet again,
We may enjoy creating memories.

As I Am

What am I without your embrace?
What am I at all?
Am I at all?

I fail to exist without your arms,
I am ignorant without your tongue,
I am lame without your legs,
I am blind without your eyes,
I am miserable without your heart,
I am poor without your hair,
I am naked without your lips.

So long as I am without you,
I am not.
So long as I am without you,
I fail.

You have taught me love,
How to pour it out,
How to drink it,
And must I not know you?
Must I live without my love?
Must I live without my love's love?
Must my heart break for love?
Must my heart break my love's love?

Do you hate me?
How have I wronged you?
Why are you far from me?
Why can't I hold you?
I die for your scent,
I live for your taste,

My heart breaks for your attention,
I need your laugh,
For your voice is as medicine,
And I am still by it.
As a river flowing through a forest,
Or as a pond,
You are rightfully placed,
And your sound,
It is as perfect as the stars at night.

My love,
My wife,
The spirit of my person,
I am tired,
I am terribly hurt,
I am without thought.
I pass away for my lacking,
I see no thing,
Good or bad,
Yet I feel all things,
And am tired.

If I could have you,
If I could know your warmth,
My soul would have its shower,
My mind would recover.
If I could have you,
If I could know your inwards,
My heart would be instructed,
My organs would be blessed.
Therefore give me your time,

And your hand,
Lend it to me,
Because I waste myself for love,
I cut my self for affection,
I slay me for compassion,
I chain you up for sorrow.

Your love is not my love,
But your love is better,
It is better in love,
Which is why I need your love,
To the end I may love me,
And not as I wish,
But as ought.

O my wife,
My beloved heart,
Although I am covered in blood,
I am clean by your tears,
And although my flesh boils,
I am right by your kiss.

My wife,
The mother of my children,
Forgive my wrong,
Ignore my smell,
But as I am,
Have me,
Come to me,
Because I am tired,
I am hurt.

Appear

Do you know I dream of you?
You are,
Repeatedly,
The subject of my dreams.

Why do you tease me?
Do you hate me?
Or maybe,
By the impression of your revelation,
I hate my self,
And do not know it.

Your face,
Your eyes,
Your lips,
Your hair,
Is warm,
And when I embrace them,
I have new life.

Your skin,
Your touch,
Your color,
Your smell,
Your taste,
Is all I want to know,
And when I embrace them,
I am alive.

My wife,
You are so cruel to me,
For you are where I am not,
But when I meet you,
And when time reaches reality,
Then you will know my love,
How deep it runs,
And how full it is.

Get in my realm.
I demand that you show your self.
I order you out of my vision;
I claim you this day;
As a body to penetrate,
And to impregnate,
And as a mind to find comfort in,
And to be edified therewith.

I love you.
I love you,
And with all that I am.

Don't lie to me.
Come to me,
My love,
My affection,
My spouse,
My kin.
Don't lie to me any more;
Make your bed with me.

Return

I love you.

As pathetic as language is,
And as incomplete,
I can only,
To convey my affection intelligently,
Say so little of what I do mean.

Can you hear me calling for you?
Can you hear my crying?
Why then do I feel you?
Is not my cry a response to a prayer?
Is not that feeling a foreshadowing conduit?
My God,
I feel her;
I feel the mother of my children;
I do not hide my heart from the vision.

My God,
Revisit my prayer.
Match my thoughts and my feelings to hers,
To her thoughts and feelings,
That we two may be one form.
I am preparing a house for you;
I have a house for you;
I am home;
Don't tease me with your presence,
But rest under my wings.

I love you.
My God,
My Wisdom,
I love her.
To the breaking of my bones,
To the fire in my spirit,
To the shattering of my profile,
To the changing of my face,
I love her,
And will love her until I die,
And until I become the key of life.

Don't look at me with those eyes,
Or with that immaculately soft and colored skin,
Press up against me.
Don't advise me from those lips;
Don't fall into my vision;
If you don't want affection,
Or if you will lie.

My Father,
Do you hate me?
Am I not broken enough?
Must you show me life,
And its pleasure,
Only to place me under vanity's spell,
That I may die in ignorance?

Do you talk and not do?
Have you spoken and not done?
Have you revealed and not educated?
Have you not both thought and acted?

Why then do you kill me?
Why do you set my thoughts so high,
Only to let the clouds choke me?
Am I not broken enough?
Is it fair to see her,
And in an untouchable realm,
Only to awake without her,
And lonely?

May tears purchase your heart?
May weeping buy attention?
How have you made me see her face,
Yet have given me liars in her place.

Is it you that hates me,
My God,
Or do I hate my self?

When,
My wife,
Will you return to me,
Because I am sick over love from you.
End,
My God,
The examination:
My faith is strong;
My heart is weak;
My body is cold;
My love burns.

Waiting

Come to me,
My love,
Into my "now,"
Into my present;
How long must I wait?

Maybe you don't feel me.
Maybe I don't resonate with your frequency.
Maybe my approach is wrong,
Or maybe my call is weak;
Because I cry over you,
Over love,
Until I collapse.

Is it not you,
My love,
Who is to resurrect me?
Is it not you who strengthens?
Why do I rant,
Why am I so heartbroken,
Why am I so lonely,
If my expectation has failed?
I am broken by my expectation,
And I am tired of waiting;
I am sick of love,
Needing nourishment.

I would take my eyes if I could,
But I know that what I see,
Despite what appears,
That it is but a lie,
And that few define love.

If I should believe my sight,
That many are found in love,
Then I would deceive my self,
Because what is found is cursed,
But what is approached,
That is blessed.
And so I wait for your approach,
And not knowing right from wrong,
I wait.

I have forced a love before,
And have known only conflict from it,
Yet what I have never forced,
That has felt right,
Giving me comfort and assurance.
Should I force love,
I should force an object of affection,
But should I wait,
I am become an object of affection,
And for the purpose of returning that love.

Come to me,
My love,
Into my "now,"
Because I need your arms,
And I can feel that mine are desired.
Have mercy on me,
Lest I am unmerciful on my self.
My love,
Return my cry to me;
Why should our prayer remain unacknowledged?

Continue

My simple foundation,
My heart's wisdom,
My love for you is above human,
My chain for you is stronger than brass and iron.

Talk to me,
Sit down with me,
I've known you since my youth,
You alone can reach me.

Do not separate from this one,
This one you've known since a youth,
Since a youth in understanding.
She is your lens.
She is your framework.
Her body of information is your playground.
Grow with her,
And if you will do well,
She will grow with you.

I have known my wife since a child in science.
Her Guardian,
As a gift,
And out of respect,
Gave her to me,
To keep,
To counsel,
And to nourish,
That by my compassion towards her,
We may be comfortable with sheets,
And with having children in bed.
Because I have failed her,

She will never fail me,
But remains beside me,
Transforming my attention,
Enlightened by my affection.

You who are sent to me,
You who strengthens me,
My loyalty to you is real.
I will be consistent in love,
I will be honest in devotion,
You can depend on my joy,
Like as my sorrow will be logical.
My tenderheartedness will be steady,
My thoughts on your body will never change,
You can expect pleasure from my eyes,
Like as my desire will be persistent.

Have I neglected you?
Have I forgotten my responsibility to you?
If I have,
You have never mentioned it,
But do silently continue with me,
Giving me your hand,
And your time,
With chance.

I can admit that I am tossed,
Tossed this way and that way,
By life,
And by failed expectation,
And although I have forgotten home,
I have never forgotten who you are.

You let my cry in the season of tears,
You join me in success in the season of alignment,
You do not encroach upon my existence,
Nor are you too far from reality,
But are reasonable in the space that you give,
Your lips ever available for good and bad times.

I am blessed to have you,
And am blessed to know you.
You return my love without apprehension.
Because you suppose love,
Because you assume possibility,
You give your self in all seasons of life,
Never courting depression when I fail to notice.

My wife,
The joy of my world,
The key to my knowledge,
I love you above love,
And I respect you above reverence.
Satiate my spirit in your arms,
Hide me in your chest,
Give me your legs,
Warm my face with your face,
That I may be sharp in understanding,
Kindly reliable.

You

My love,
Show you.

It isn't good to leave affection without release;
It isn't good live without knowledge.
Be my knowledge,
Receive my affection,
That we both may be fulfilled,
That we both may be content.

Is marriage too difficult?
Is companionship unnecessary?
Why can I then feel your cry,
But you cannot feel mine?

Maybe I am too proud.
Or maybe I am not humble enough.
There is more to life than love,
Than being sick of love,
For where there is a knowledge of love,
Therein is found love's cure.

How then can I radiate my affection to you?
What sound can I give?
My thoughts and feelings bring me to you,
And we spend the night embracing.

I have cried for your presence;
Give me your voice.
I have cried for your consolation;
Lay on me.
Your character is a proverb;
Your person is a hymn;
Your soul is a psalm;
Let me inside of your hidden part,
That I may know how to better love myself.

What then have I done to you?
Why am I so invisible to your prayer?
Should I see you,
When I find you,
As I have you,
You will finally see me,
And we will be our last memory,
Time concluding what chance begun.

Love Me

Sit and pray with me,
My love.

Fellowship with me,
Communicate your heart to me,
My wife,
And let me mature in love.

You will never know,
Never know how much of a joy it is to see your face,
To see your face every morning,
Every evening,
Every night.

Because of you our home is warm,
Because of you our home is simple,
Because of you our home is peace,
Because of you our home is intelligent.
And you know my struggle,
My struggle to possess a home,
And so you make every household burden light,
You keep me apprised to alleviation and conscious of affection.

Let me die between your breasts,
Regenerate me by your lips,
Command my attention by your walk,
Nourish me by your communion's shower.
Because I am not wise,
And when it comes to wit,
I am more stubborn than discreet.

Talk to me of kindness,
Inform me of betterment,
Convert me to reflection,
Teach me how to kiss,
Lay me down between your breasts,
And give me the key to your chest.

I wish you knew how jealous time is of me.
Because we are together,
Time is mad,
Not knowing where to leave off,
For I have forgotten about it,
Through you.
You, then, are timeless,
And your age cannot be defined,
Yet your speech is the revelation of a woman,
Of a woman dipped in wisdom and washed with empathy.

I am so thankful to you for my home,
And for my home's atmosphere.
I have seen a virtuous woman,
And a virtuous woman has let me inside of her,
To know the temperament of the edified,
And to know the patience of the forgiven.

I love you in the morning,
And at night my love is refreshed,
For the same eyes,
From start to finish,
Look on me.
I wish you knew how beautiful your eyes are,
And also your legs,

I am a man by their spreading,
I am a son by their gape,
And am honored by their sincerity,
And by the honest continuance of their affinity.

Love me,
My wife,
Every morning and every evening,
Because I am,
Outside of our walls,
Hated.

Love me,
My Queen,
Every morning and every evening,
Because my parents have passed away,
And their room is vacant.

Love me,
My love,
Every morning and every evening,
Because I love love,
And because I love the taste of your love,
When we fellowship,
And when we commune.

I Prayed

What can I say to express my self?
What can I say to reveal my feelings?

I am at loss for words,
Am without language,
To articulate your presence,
And your worth,
To my mind.

I am taken by your effect,
And by your hold,
On me.
If you should never write back,
I am as a ship tossed by the wind,
For I live by the hope that I have in us,
And I have faith in the wisdom that you are.

Truly I am sick of love,
And am unable to speak,
Being tormented by the joy of affection.
I hate having no knowledge to express my self,
I hate having no thought to portray my delight,
But if I could,
Would my experience be honest?
If I could tell you my heart,
Would my love be genuine?

I have prayed for love,
I had faith that she would find me,
I knew that she would,
And yet,
I am taken by surprise at it.

I prayed for a wife,
I had faith that she would find me,
And I knew that she would,
Yet I am taken by surprise that she is here.

There is a force that hears our cry,
There are invisible Eyes that see,
And they are seen when blind.
Our cry is heard,
Our supplication is considered,
When thought and feeling are combined,
Or when will and emotion marry.

What,
Then,
Can be said for the expected unexpected occurrence?
I have no words to tell of its magnitude,
Like as I have no idea of her depth.
She loves me more than I love her,
Yet I love her more,
Because of the spirit that created her.

Acknowledgment

Find me,
My love,
According to my voice,
And according to my call,
Find me,
And be found of me.

Be found of me,
Reveal your self,
Show your face,
That I may know my prayers are heard,
And that my frequency,
Into the world of our force,
And into the universe of our desire,
Resonates.

Do you not want companionship?
Is not your cry for union?
Aren't you ready for motherhood?
Don't you have time?

Are you afraid of me?
Isn't a relationship trouble?
But aren't we made of love?
Don't we both love a challenge?

Find me,
My love,
Find me right now,
Because I am ready for life.

To what end do I wait?
What am I wiring for?
And you,
If marriage is your prayer,
Must you hide from me,
Or must you take you away from vision?

Act on your prayers.
Move through your supplication.
Our voice has penetrated the heavens:
When I look up,
I will see the one I have created,
Who is also the one I am created for.

I am tired of waiting,
I am tired of love,
I am sick of not living.
Refrain from hiding,
Show yourself,
You who so boldly prays for a husband,
And yet,
Will not think to embrace revelation.

Open your eyes and see,
See that I am here,
Because I see you,
And only pray for acknowledgment.

An End

Is there an end to love?
Is there an end to science?
There is an end to success,
To depression,
To hunger,
To allure,
To joy,
But for love,
Is there an end?

My journey has given fame.
A rise from obscurity is amusement,
And for the curious,
It is noise for attention.
To sell many books,
To speak at every place,
Is to fulfill a reason,
But for love,
What can compete?

My love,
Who is the spirit of my birth,
Is also my end.
I have called,
She has answered.
She has called,
I have answered.
It would seem as though our matrimony is the end,
The end of knowledge,
Of commitment,
Of pleasure,
Of confidence,

Which is why I question its end.

My love,
I see no departure from you.
Though I don't understand you,
And believe I never will,
I see our course of learning lasting for ever,
With death being the start of our perfect beginning.

In every regeneration of life,
I will find you.
Let us quit this age and take on another:
I will find you.
There is only one answer to our call,
And although we may spend years apart,
Our cycling through garbage will reveal our bond,
Promoting our end.

Though my time with you is short,
I will find you again.
This earth can only hold one fragrance for you and I,
And that fragrance can only unite you and I.
If I could kill the men that had you before me,
I would,
Or if I could be the first,
I would,
And as the last,
I would remind you that I am yours,

And I would show you how it feels to be loved.

I love you.

I apologize for my ignorance,
I am sorry for my wrong,
And being naturally unhealthy,
I thank you for only seeing my virtue.

I love you.

To learn how to educate my love is my joy,
And to receive correction from you is a pleasure,
Awakening my person to an end it was born for.

Clarification

How short is time?
This life,
It is nothing,
And the time encapsulating it,
It is nothing at all,
But a witness to the fact that we should live,
That we should live wisely in and with love,
For so long as we are limited by time,
And for so long as we will.

And this is the lesson that you have taught me:
That a certain will is joined to life.
To have that will,
It is to have life's intelligence catering to our mind.
Because we first accept subjection to life's mind,
Because we would be regulated by life's spirit,
Because we would listen to life,
For our obedience,
Wisdom is given to beautify our experience,
And knowledge to color our vision.

Because you make life livable,
You make life wonderful.
The pain of circumstance,
The aggravation of stimulus,
The joy of abuse,
The exhaustion of sorrow,
Is perfected by wisdom,
And is hushed by understanding,
That I may see you,
And that I may discern your worth.

I can't,
Anymore,
Think on what to feel sorry over.
You have clarified my mind,
And have cleared the conscience of my person,
That I may enjoy me,
And that I may also discern your worth.

Yet there is,
But not really,
A downside to your presence.
You add consciousness,
So now being conscious,
I feel more, and do truly observe more.

There is pain when observing more.
Before you, I observed less,
And felt neither joy nor sorrow.
Yet knowledge distorts environment,
And that distortion, although blessed,
Is but an aggravation of the heart's chord.

So do I think your effect is bad?
Should I?
Maybe if I was another man.

If I was another man,
I couldn't take your revelation.
But I am lucky that I am me,
And that my inquiry is into my self,
Because I value you,
Who is my spirit,

Rare

Your light and dark hair,
Your thick and soft skin,
Your sure and intelligent hands and feet,
Your strong legs,
Your nourishing breasts,
Your wise lips,
Your understanding eyes,
The rare shape and structure of your form,
The course of your tongue,
The benevolence of your thighs,
The comfort of your arms,
Means nothing to the essence of your person,
Or the revelation of your disposition,
The beauty of your individuality,
The allure of your mind.

I love you,
My love,
I love every part of you.

I love you,
My spirit,
My soul's greater portion;
I love every part of you,
And I love what you are not.

Isn't this love?
Have you never edified me?
Have I never seen who you are?
Am I ignorant of your ugliness?
Have you never let me understand you?
That you are complicated because you love,

My dedication to you is authentic,
My devotion to your lips is real,
Because although you are imperfect,
You remember my frailty,
And because of your response to your weakness,
And of your thoughts towards my condition,
I am inclined to make your existence lighter,
And to edify my self on how to do so.

Love works;
Love balances;
If we never took turns engaging humility,
We would fail.
But more than the feeling of pain,
And of embarrassment,
Is the memory of pain,
And the memory of embarrassment,
Watering the heart to sprout a garden of mindfulness,
Keeping the person aware of love.

You are rare because of your love's spirit.
Your love is developed,
Your love is recovering,
Your affection is genuine,
You naturally care.
I admire you,
My love,
I admire you,
Because of your thoughtful generosity.

Where can a man find such a woman?
What man has such a woman?

Under the earth,
You won't see her.
If looking above the earth,
You will be deceived.
If born without her,
You have no hope.

I died with you,
And when you awoke,
You put your mouth on mine,
And your hand,
Ever so gently,
On my face,
And gave me your breath,
Opening my eyes,
And made love to me.

But what is greater than death's sensation?
What is greater than warmth?
What about the memory of your spouse,
How imperfect they are,
To console their error?
Isn't this true comfort?
Isn't this what love is made of?

How am I mindful of this,
And no other man is?
How am I mindful of this,
And no other woman is?

Everywhere,
And in every place,
There are women,
Yet not one of them knows the meaning of humility.
Everywhere,
And in every place,
There are women,
And none are wise to love.
The species born to love,
And born to feel,
And more than their opposite,
Do not know,
Or have no knowledge on,
True,
And timeless,
Affection.

My heart is broken.

My heart is broken for earth's condition,
Because where there are no women,
There is no sound counsel.
I have seen many women,
And yet continue to do so,
And with all that I have seen,
From every place,
None know the meaning of being still,
Being compromised by a love within their nature.

But when I look at you,
My love,
I can see that you are rare,
Being no different from what I do see,
But being mindful of your nature,
To instruct it.
Because you instruct you,
You can instruct me,
And because I learn from you,
I can be who I truly am,
So that you can never be ashamed of what you are.

My wife,
Feel my love,
And continually regenerate.
Show your face,
And let me love you.
Let me love you because you love you,
Let me love you because I love me,
Let's make love because we are love,
And let's create love because we are spirit.

Union

What is better than love?
What is better than edification?
Life is complex,
And the human being insecure,
But what can compare to love,
And to the experience of edification?

In you,
My love,
I have found my end.
I have found,
In you,
My spirit,
My fate,
That I am to be sick in love,
And searching for consolation.

What is nature to prediction?
What is assumption to imagination?
Must I yet hope and never know?
Must I quarrel for nothing?
Must I be so near to love that I cannot have it?
Must I suffer myself to die alone?

What is wrong with me?
Am I as distorted as I imagine?
Or has time and chance given up on me?
Must I miss the beauty of communion?
Must I take my seed to the grave?

If love is as confused as life,
Surely we have a happy home.
Remain,
Keep your faith,
And let it water the garden of my person.
Though differences separate,
Let them bring us closer,
And though love hurts,
Let it edify our marriage.

Though love hurts,
Share its liberty with me.
We don't know tomorrow,
And we could love others,
But we are born in this love,
And if born,
Then we are created for its challenge.

I know love to be only edifying,
And my experience with love to be only disappointing.
Let go with me,
My love,
And chase away the pain of the unknown,
Because the present isn't fate,
But is only determining union.

Consider

Your form,
Must it be so elegant?
Must your symmetry be idyllic?
Must your grace sing?
Must you radiate femininity?
Must your spirit be so lovely?

Is there a man luckier than I?
I am horrified when our eyes meet,
Because I am not as harmonious,
And because I am not as sure.

But you observe me.
You already know my faults.
You fall on me,
You share your aura with me,
You let me in,
You accept my romance.

Your placement is divine.
Life heard my prayers,
And opened up,
Giving me a creature,
And a wife to fecundate.

May I shower you?
May I drench you in love?
If you have blessed me,
Should I not edify you?

Your brilliance is irrational.
Your essence makes no sense.
How one woman may house such a character

To control a well-informed energy,
Is the greatest mystery I have ever known.

Yet,
I am the only one to discover it.
She is given to no other man,
And would have no other,
But I.
Her care is for me to know,
And she would have it as is,
But I am still in awe,
Over what I have done to receive this honor,
Because I am clueless.

Am I wrong to question?
Am I wrong to prod?
Often she tells me to shut up,
And to kiss her.
Often she tells me she loves me,
And she shows it,
By considering my nature.

Know

You are addition,
And good multiplication.
You are not division,
Or subtraction.
You have changed me:
My behavior is wise,
My mind is composed,
My feelings are mature,
My thoughts are able.

Your allure is categorized as wisdom,
It is identified as understanding.
The intellect of your heart instructs,
And with every interaction,
I am corrected,
I am edified,
I am counseled,
I am bettered.

So although I cry,
Tasting many tears,
And although I sleep,
For fear of waking more error,
I may smile.
Because of you,
I smile,
And because of you,
I bottle much sorrow.

And I must be lucky,
Or at least fortunate,
Because you ask for every bottle of sorrow,
And I give,
Disinterested in what is done with them.
It is as if you hold the book of my prayers,
And burn it,
Alleviating my person,
Making life bearable.

My priestess,
My wife,
Why do you enjoy putting my temple in order?
How is my home your concern?
You will to create within me,
Being honorable in your desire,
And majestic in your operation.
Because it is as if,
Through purchasing beauty,
Through decorating fascination,
Through reprimanding love,
Through order,
Your care has increased,
Along with your fondness for me.
You govern my temple and increase in love,
Giving me your self,
Sacrificing your organs on the altar of my affection.

Never have I smelled love before,
But now I do.
Never have I tasted affection,
But now I cooperate with it.

You are silent for me,
You behave for me,
You justify for me,
You create for me,
And are forgiving me,
All for nothing I've done,
Or at least for what I cannot discern.

Is this love?
Am I within love?
Recall our frustration,
Remember our fights,
Rehearse the pain we cause each other,
And wonder about love.
Because where has it all gone?
Why are we at peace?

What then is love's "sin"?
Is it separation?
Is the death of love misunderstanding?
When apart,
We were bad,
But now,
Sharing a home,
We are still,
We communicate,
We learn,
We are equally teachable.

What is this love?
What is this experience?
Because it surely is no emotion,
But is senseless,
Abusive,
Benevolent,
Wise,
Comforting.

You have added love.
You are the first,
And I have made you the last.
You have added love to my life,
Making me aware of my person,
Returning to my nature its lost sensitivity.
You have taught me that love is knowledge,
And that to love,
Is to know.

Know with me,
My love,
Love's light.
Know with me,
My wife,
Love's constellation.
Give me knowledge of love,
And I will never leave you,
And the confession of love,
And I will return it.

Know with me,
My love,
Every part of love.
I am sick of love,
I am overcome with affection,
Needing one to shower,
Needing one to console.

Time and chance have therefore pitied me,
Giving me my prayer.
They grew tired of hearing me,
They grew tired of my pathetic plea,
As I destroyed my self to their mind,
And became a beast to their understanding.

Is this what moves them?
Do they like a broken heart?
I must admit so,
Because they returned an apology,
And in a most elegant form,
According to the words of my supplication.

This they did,
I believe,
For knowledge,
And for knowing the height of existence,
That I may better my nature,
From bettering hers.

To Wisdom

"Sit,"
She says,
"With me.

"What's wrong?"
She says,
"Why are you sad?
You're ok.
Even though you're uncomfortable,
You're ok.

"Don't think about what you don't have,
Or where you are not.
The treasure for that time is for that time,
But consider the present.
You think you're out of place,
And you think you know better,
And you think you are alone,
And you think you are born limited,
But what if,
Instead of thinking,
You lived?

"Maybe you are right,
That who is within is not correctly placed in time.
And maybe you are right,
That loneliness is all that you should expect.
But what about this present experience?
What about the knowledge you have from these feelings?
What about your lens?
What about the ability you now have to live better?

"If you were practical,
Don't you think life would be better?
If you applied to wisdom,
Don't you think that life would be lenient?
Should you keep mourning over you?
Should you die?
What if you cared for "now"?
Should you then receive what is expected?

"What if the day didn't care for the sun?
Or what if the night didn't care for the moon?
Would the day receive the sun?
Or would the night receive the moon?
Should the day receive the sun?
Or should the sun,
If the day didn't think to care for its self,
Think to occupy the day,
So that the day could receive it?
What if the day failed to care for its self?
Should it be worthy of the sun?
Should the sun even think that the day is worthy of it?
Or should the sun,
Exercising kindness,
Not wait until the day is ready for it?

"So you,
My love,
Do you think that,
If you do not care for today,
And the person you are today,
The life you anticipate,
And the person you expect to be,

Don't you think that,
If you can presently learn gratefulness,
That you will soon see contentment's return?

"The day,
And the sun,
With the night,
And the moon,
Exercise humility.
My love,
Are you humble?

"You cannot rule life.
Life does not accept government.
Its own law governs it,
And don't you think that,
If you learned humility,
To take knowledge of that law,
That life would take knowledge of you,
That you are fit to receive the return of humility?

"My love,
It's not what you want to hear,
But what you need to know.

"You need to know that you are rare,
And that life loves you.
You need to know that life sees you,
And that life hears you,
And that life doesn't care about what it senses,
But about who or what will learn humility.

So feel alone and be frustrated,
Feel tired and be lost,
Drink the wine of your tears,
And eat the bread of your bones,
But never forget to do so intelligently,
Or without receiving correction to better understand.

"And never forget that you have my love.
I alone am given to you by life.
You are,
Upon birth,
Guaranteed only three things:
Death; life; me.
You are not alone.
Yes, we are young,
Learning growth,
But I will love you.
But I need you to love you,
Because if you don't love you,
How can you love me?

"Why are you sad?
I understand what you feel,
And I will never deny you that pain,
But,
My love,
You are missing today,
And are missing me.

"Love me.
Give all of you to me,
And love me.
Forget about it all,
And love me.
If you will be cruel,
Be cruel to me,
Because then we may create love,
If we are not too sick of it."

Stop

"What if I alone knew about your fame?"
She says.
"What if I only knew your spirit?
Would that be wrong?
Would it be "sin"?
Is that too simple?
Or is it too unrealistic?

"What if,
Ignoring every thing,
You let our family grow?
What if you didn't handle life?
What if you didn't force revelation?
Is it wrong to live without pressure?
Have you gained from harassing you?
Isn't it better to live in simplicity,
Having no imaginary rank to climb?

"But it's real to you.
There is nothing imaginary about what you see.
But how long will you let a vision kill you?
Should a thought ruin you?
If a thought of life is unforced,
Should not the life of life be unforced?
Why can't you see what you have,
And not what you don't,
To live wise,
So that you may live on in memories?

"Family is everything.
My love,
Have a family with me.

Give your family your spirit.
Let the world care for itself,
And let life care for you,
But give your family your spirit,
Enjoy your children,
Don't be so serious,
And life will see.

"The willing suffers many sorrows.
Are you losing time?
Are you forgetting something?
My love,
Be sick of love.
My love,
Worry about what you can control,
Because what you can't control,
Does think to be ever mindful of you.

"Do I have to see you like this?
You are better than sorrow,
Yet you won't see.

"Listen,
My husband,
To your wife,
Who is also your spirit.

"Let go.
Stop.
Enjoy what you have,
And where you are,
For contentment today,
And for your legacy to come."

Say

If it is you,
Just say it is you.

If it is you,
Don't pretend.

I am alive for love,
I have been preserved for family,
I am trained to be a father,
I am kept to be a husband.

If you will forgive me,
My love,
Hear my prayer,
And forgive me.
If you will love me,
My love,
Hear my prayer,
And love me.
All my life has been spent in sorrow,
But if it is you that I see,
If you have heard my call,
And are here for marriage,
Then come to me,
Then forgive me,
And kiss me.

Is it you?
Are you deceiving me?
You know I am sick of love,
And you know that I am ready for marriage.
Don't lie to me.

Let me acknowledge you,
Let me absorb you,
Let me know you,
For who you are,
And for why you are here.

I am dying for your love.
I am tired of calling,
And of being lied to.
It is you,
After every prayer,
That I now see,
Standing before me,
With your love displayed,
Wearing your imperfection.

I am dying for love.
I am dying for marriage,
For a free communion,
Without hindrance,
Between mind and body.

Why fight me?
Why manipulate perception?
What is gained from arguing?
What is gained when resisting affection?
Who are we to fight nature?
Who are we to fight wisdom?

Stop lying to me.

I am too intelligent for craft,
Yet I am not old enough for

I am too wise for foolishness,
Yet I am not old enough for delusion.
Stop lying to me,
Because I lie to me,
And I am already oppressed.
If you are not here,
Just tell me.
Tell me to stop looking,
Tell me to stop feeling,
Tell me to stop asking,
Tell me to stop doing.
If you are not here,
Cut the chord of simplicity,
But if you are here,
If it is you,
Then let me love you,
Let me die for you,
Let me cry with you,
Let me show you who I am.

I can't live,
Anymore,
Being sick of love.
I am beyond passion,
I am above amiability,
I am tired of having no wisdom,
And no sense,
Of the love that I am.
And I am tired of you,
My love,
For not letting you exist to me,
And me to you.

If it is you,
Just say it is you.

If it is you,
Then talk.

The language of the soul,
And the iteration of affection,
Is without word and deed,
But confession moves.

If it is you,
Just say it is you,
Because I hope that it is.

Growth

I have deceived myself of my worth,
Of my beauty,
Of my condition.

I have lied to me about love,
About ambition,
About vision.

Yet you remain.
You see beyond the mess,
The mess that I am,
To coordinate your affection,
So that you don't have to leave,
Even if it is what you desire.

You wonder why I die for you,
You wonder why I stress over us,
You wonder why I don't listen,
When such a love overwhelms me.
You think I don't know,
You think I can't perceive,
But I do,
And am not afraid to ignore what is,
So that I may have what should be.

Because, what is life?
What is this?
It is a repetitive sitcom that never tires.
It is an unfolded tragedy unfolding anew.
It is nothing desirable,
But,
Because of you,

I live for you.
I love for you.
I am broken for you.
I resurrect for you.
I expect for you.
I am patient for you.
I am lenient for you.
I starve for you.
I am buried for you.
I circulate for you.

I know injury for you.
I desire virtue because of you.
I am a man through you.
I will argue for you.
I am humble for you.
I am quiet for you.
I look ahead because of you.
For you,
I have forgotten the past.

The life of a man is contemplative,
But you have made this experience peaceful.
You remain through my ignorance,
You adjust to my insolence,
You console my fever,
You renew my spirit.

My wife,
Where would I be without you?
I would be stagnant,
And I would know only compression,
If I did not have you.
But I know growth,
And only growth,
From your kiss,
Which is your embrace.

See

Is honesty too much?
Am I wrong to care for your belief?
Am I wrong to demand your appearance?
If you will have me,
Then have me,
If you will appear,
Then show,
And tell me that you are here,
And that I am not asleep.

I have never denied my defect.
I have never told you that I am whole.
But now you know,
You know how I am known,
And how I am sorry for me,
Because now you have evidence,
Evidence of my humanity,
Evidence of my frailty,
Evidence of my ignorance,
Of my insecurity,
Of my character.

How long have I waited for you?
How much longer must I wait?
Must circumstance dictate so much?
Must time mock chance?

How am I ready,
Yet not my life?
How am I here,
Yet not my life?

Because of me,
I am fallen into despair,
Yet,
In this tragedy,
You remain,
And giving the entire half that you are,
Or that you are willing to give.

This kills me,
That you would give me your love,
And show me all of you,
Yet only giving half of all,
Revealing only half of the vision.
I am coarse,
And in tone and presence,
Imperfect;
Is this enough for you to stop yourself?
How unbearable am I?

I,
As I ought,
Do not know my faults.
I,
As I ought,
Cannot see me.
But I feel my sorrow.
So should a seed,
Outside of soil,
Expect to grow?
I have but recently found ground,
And must I think to grow so soon?

Will you accept me as I am?
Will you respect me as I am?
Will you let me respect you?
Will you let me accept you?
Do you even care,
Care that I am sick of love?
Can you see that when you don't,
When you don't give you,
Our communion is broken?
Is our embrace nothing?
Is our struggle pointless?
Do we stress for profession only?
Do you,
My love,
Even care that I hate the sight of me?

Do you have no good thoughts of me?
How do I look?
If I have ruined me to you,
Why haven't you talked to me,
Or why haven't you asked what's wrong?
Aren't you tired of guessing?
Can't you see that you hurt yourself?
Why think about what may be,
When you can know what is?

Can you hear me?
Can you hear me calling to you?
If you can see me,
Just see me,

But if I will only be monstrous,
And injurious,
To you,
Inform me of myself,
Because I am sick of love,
And of your love.

I need you.
I need you to hear me.
I need you to hear my prayer,
And I need you to give me yours.
I need you to know that I am ready,
I need you to know that I am here,
I need you to stop praying for me,
And to see that I am here.

I exist.
I need you to know that I exist.
I need your faith.
I need you to know that I am here,
And that I exist,
Only for you.

I need you to stop feeling for me,
And to begin to touch me.
I need you to stop thinking about me,
And to love me;
I need you with me.

A man without his woman is incomplete.
A man without his woman is without life.

Why can't you just accept that I am here,
That I am your husband,
And that I am here,
And have been waiting for you to see me?

Why can't you see me?
Why can't you see who I am?
Why can't you respect your sight?
Why do you think so ill of me?

Why can't you see me?
Why can't you just look?
Why can't you just understand,
That I am here,
And that I am your husband?

Do you think I will ruin you?
Do you think I am harmful?
I will admit that,
I am injurious to my self,
But to you,
Why should I be?
Why must you think so low of me?
Why not give me your faith?

Do you know how broken I am?
Do you even care?

Let me materialize.
I need you to see me.

Exist

Can you see me?
Do you care to know me?
How have I wronged you?
Why can't you acknowledge me?

I take no pride in the sight of my self.
I understand I am imperfect,
And that in my imperfection,
I am fairly well,
But why do I,
And not you,
Have this mentality?

What if you could observe you?
What if you could take knowledge of you?
What if you saw disfigurement?
Would you heal?
Would you suffer?

How is it that you,
Being enlightenment,
Are yet ignorant?
How,
Being sober,
Are you yet heavily inebriated?

I can see that you love,
And that you are love,
Yet you cannot,
And I cannot understand why.
The beauty of your growth is wise,
Showing the disease of humanity,

You are so magnificent,
But because you cannot see it,
You are without correction,
Having no regard,
No perception.

Yet I am not altogether removed from vision.
You have made me your business,
And our relationship your sanctuary.
You run into my arms,
Resting on my chest,
Your energy pouring into my portal,
Deciding the landscape of my affection.
You are safe in my arms,
You are known,
You are loved,
But I am still unknown,
Even as we touch.

My love,
I need you to see me.
Because my nature is unsympathetic,
I need your consolation,
I need your lips,
I need you to see me.

My love,
If I am not whole,
Do not take advantage.
My nature,
Being unsympathetic,
Is yet not irredeemable.

I am here to stay,
I am here to learn,
I am here to fight for love,
And to know how we defines us.
Hear my prayers and let your heart exist,
Because I need you to see me,
So that I can know what is real.

There is a triumph in love,
Even an unspoken fellowship.
You are my prayer,
You are the reality of a female,
And to possess a memory of time with you,
It is to possess wealth,
And to garner every bit of earth's fame.

I am content with you in my arms,
As the center of my affection,
And as the soil for my seed.
Let yourself see me,
And come to me,
So that we may know eternity,
And the pressure of few.

Return

You are my strength.
Know your benefit,
And your worth,
To my existence.

Life can distract,
And emotions can ferment thought,
But I can never forget you.
I have done wrong to our fellowship,
I have damaged our communion,
I have ignored intercourse,
Because of this and because of that,
And because of them and because of those,
But I have not forgotten us,
Nor will I ever.

I am never unfaithful,
Or unbelieving,
But I am asleep,
And am tragically ignorant.
I am a terror to my self,
And having none other to cry with,
I,
At my lowest,
Turn to you,
And you accept me.

How long will you ignore my self-righteousness?
How long will you continue to console me?
If you should refrain,
I would die.
If you never opened up your arms,

And through all of my foolishness,
As a wife,
A friend,
A counselor,
And mother.

Why is this so hard to say?
Why is love never enough?
I can say that I have grown through conflict,
And am more intelligent because of hardship,
Yet my eyes are still closed to your brilliance,
And my heart to your wisdom.

All things fail,
And all things come with regret,
But my wife,
Who is the spouse of my life,
Is my reprieve.

My wife,
I am taken by who you are.
We were brought together in youth,
And were married in innocence,
By your father,
Who knew that I needed you,
And that you were created for me.

Demand my love,
Agitate me for affection,
Because I don't know who I am,
And am at loss at the sight of my form,
Needing a reminder of who I ought to be.